First
Facts®

FACT FILE

CONTINENTS

What You Need to Know

by JILL SHERMAN

CAPSTONE PRESS
a capstone imprint

First Facts are published by Capstone Press,
1710 Roe Crest Drive, North Mankato, Minnesota 56003
www.mycapstone.com

Library of Congress Cataloging-in-Publication Data
Library of Congress Cataloging-in-Publication data is available on the Library of Congress website.
ISBN 978-1-5157-8110-3 (library binding)
ISBN 978-1-5157-8124-0 (paperback)
ISBN 978-1-5157-8131-8 (eBook PDF)

Editorial Credits
Mandy Robbins, editor; Jenny Bergstrom, designer; Kelly Garvin, media researcher; Laura Manthe, production specialist

Photo Credits
Shutterstock: Adwo, 15, (bottom left), Andrzej Kubik, 15 (middle right), Arthur Balitskiy, 5, Bardocz Peter, cover (top left, bottom right), 1, Bildagentur Zoonar GmBbH, cover (top right, bl), Bill Chariya, 19 (inset), Daniel Prudek, 8, Designua, 3, EcoPrint, 7, Filipe Frazao, 15 (tl) (br), InnervisionArt, 9, Kristian Bell, 16, LUMOimages, 12, Norimoto, 20, Olga Danylenko, 21, Phanom Nuangchomphoo, 13, pisaphotography, 22, S.Borisov, 11-12, szefei, 24, Tookrub, 17, Vaclav Volrab, 6, Vadim Petrakov, 15 (tr), Wojciech Dziadosz, 18-19

Artistic elements: Shutterstock/Mikko Lemola

Printed in China.
010295F17

Table of Contents

A Giant Landmass

Land and water cover Earth. Look at a world map. You can count seven large landmasses. They are **continents**. Each is entirely or mostly surrounded by water.

Long ago, all of Earth's land was joined. Scientists call this single landmass Pangaea. Pangaea began to drift apart about 200 million years ago. It broke into today's seven continents.

continent—one of Earth's seven large landmasses

DRIFTING
CONTINENTS

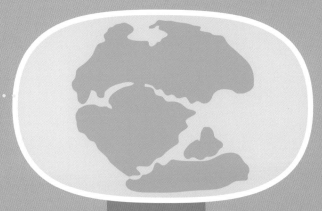

225
MILLION YEARS AGO

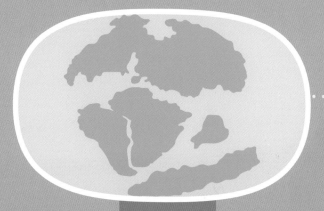

150
MILLION YEARS AGO

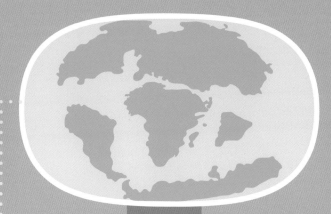

65
MILLION YEARS AGO

Present

Africa

Africa is home to the Sahara, the world's largest **desert**. It also has the longest river, the Nile. Many impressive wild animals live in Africa. They include lions, giraffes, and elephants. Most scientists agree the first humans lived in Africa too.

desert—a dry area with little rain
plateau—an area of high, flat land

AT A GLANCE:
AFRICA

SIZE

11.6
million square miles

(30 million square kilometers)

NUMBER OF COUNTRIES

54

POPULATION

more than

1

billion

Asia

Asia is Earth's largest continent. More people live there than any other continent. Asia is a land of extremes. To the north lies the frozen Arctic Ocean. In the south there are **tropical** jungles. Asia also has thick forests, large deserts, and long rivers.

FACT

The world's tallest mountain is found in Asia. It is Mount Everest.

tropical—having to do with hot and wet areas near the equator

SIZE

17.2
**million
square miles**

(44.5 million
square km)

NUMBER OF
COUNTRIES

50

POPULATION

4.5
billion

Europe

Europe is west of Asia. It is the second smallest continent. But it has a large **population**. Other continents have wide-open spaces. People occupy most of Europe.

Europe and Asia are part of the same land mass. Some scientists consider them one continent called Eurasia.

population—a group of people, animals, or plants living in a certain place

POPULATION DENSITY

Check out the average number of people living in one square mile on each continent.

SIZE

4
**million
square miles**

(10.4 million
square km)

**NUMBER OF
COUNTRIES**

> **49**

POPULATION

724
million

PEOPLE						
95	34	22	22	0	73	3

100
80
60
40
20
0

Asia | Africa | North America | South America | Antarctica | Europe | Australia

North America

North America lies across the Atlantic Ocean from Europe. It has every type of land and **climate**. There are mountains, deserts, forests, and swamps. People in northern areas live in very cold temperatures. Those in southern countries have tropical weather.

climate—average weather of a place throughout the year

NORTH AMERICA

SIZE

9.3
million
square miles

(24.1 million
square km)

NUMBER OF COUNTRIES

> **23**

POPULATION

more than
572
million

South America

South America has many natural wonders. The Amazon **rain forest** is the world's largest rain forest. The Amazon River carries 15 to 20 percent of Earth's freshwater to the ocean. Angel Falls in Venezuela is the world's highest waterfall. The Andes are the longest mountain range. The Atacama Desert is one of the hottest, driest places on Earth.

rain forest—a thick forest where rain falls almost every day

AMAZON RIVER

ANGEL FALLS

ATACAMA DESERT

AMAZON RAIN FOREST

ANDES MOUNTAINS

WATER
MOUNTAINS
DESERT
RAINFOREST

SOUTH AMERICA

SIZE

6.8
million
square miles

(17.6 million
square km)

NUMBER OF COUNTRIES

12

POPULATION

more than
418
million

15

Australia

Australia is the largest island in the world. But it is the smallest continent. Australia is also the only continent that is its own country. There are mountains and cities in the east. Western Australia is home to dry deserts and grasslands. Few people live in the west.

FACT
Australia is known to have many poisonous animals. It has more deadly snakes than any other country.

AT A GLANCE:
AUSTRALIA

SIZE

2.9
million
square miles

(7.5 million
square km)

NUMBER OF COUNTRIES

1

POPULATION

more than
24
million

17

Antarctica

Antarctica is the coldest, windiest place on Earth. An ice sheet covers the land. A few mountains rise above the ice. Without its ice, Antarctica would look much smaller.

People visit Antarctica, but no one makes it their home. Many scientists study Antarctica. It has more than 40 research stations.

ANTARCTICA

Antarctica's ice is 3 miles (4.8 km) thick in some places.

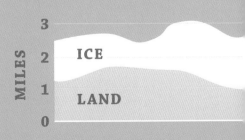

ANTARCTICA ICE SHEET AREA

LAND

ICE

Maps of Antarctica include its ice sheet. The land beneath is much smaller than what is shown on a map.

3 MILES THICK

ANTARCTICA

SIZE

5.4 ◄
million square miles

(14 million square km)

NUMBER OF COUNTRIES

⋯▸ 0

POPULATION

0 ◄⋯

VISITORS

1,000
in winter ◄⋯

4,500
in summer

Oceania

Some places are not part of any continent. About 30,000 islands dot the Pacific Ocean. They are part of an area called Oceania.

Some large islands are countries. Papua New Guinea and New Zealand are Pacific island nations. Other islands are tiny. They barely rise above the ocean's surface.

AT A GLANCE:
OCEANIA

SIZE

more than
300,000
square miles

(776,000
square km)

NUMBER OF COUNTRIES

13

POPULATION

20
million

Glossary

climate (KLY-muht)—average weather of a place throughout the year

continent (KAHN-tuh-nuhnt)—one of Earth's seven large landmasses

desert (DE-zuhrt)—a dry area with little rain

plateau (pla-TOH)—an area of high, flat land

population (pop-yuh-LAY-shuhn)—a group of people, animals, or plants living in a certain place

rain forest (RAYN FOR-ist)—a thick forest where rain falls almost every day

tropical (TRAH-pi-kuhl)—having to do with the hot and wet areas near the equator

Read More

Bullard, Lisa. *This is My Continent.* Where I Live. Minneapolis: Millbrook Press, 2017.

Cane, Ella. *Continents in My World.* My World. North Mankato, Minn.: Capstone, 2014.

Harris, Irene. *Earth's Continents.* Spotlight on Earth Science. New York: PowerKids Press, 2017.

Internet Sites

Use FactHound find Internet sites related to this book.

Visit *www.facthound.com*

Just type in 9781515781103

 Check out projects, games and lots more at **www.capstonekids.com**

Critical Thinking Questions

1. Reread pages 10 through 13. How are Europe and North America alike? How are they different?

2. Which of the continents would you most like to visit? Why?

3. Which continent is most different from the others? How is it different?

Index